EBBF

A Guide to Installing Equitable Beneficiary-Based Finance in Local Government

Anthony Pascal
With Michael Caggiano, Judith Fernandez,
Kevin McCarthy, Kevin Neels, C. Peter Rydell,
James P. Stucker

Rand

The research described was supported by the U.S. Department of Health and Human Services under Grant No. 90-CJ-56/01; by The City of Saint Paul; and by The Ford Foundation under Grant No. 730-0501. General support to The City of Saint Paul was supplied by the U.S. Department of Housing and Urban Development. Additional support was supplied by The Saint Paul Companies, The General Mills Foundation, The Saint Paul Foundation, The F. R. Bigelow Foundation, and The Otto Bremer Foundation.

Library of Congress Cataloging in Publication Data
Main entry under title:

EBBF: a guide to installing equitable beneficiary-based
    finance in local government.

    "R-3124-HHS/SP/FF."
    1. User charges—United States.   2. Local finance—United
States. I. Pascal, Anthony H.   II. United States.
Dept. of Health and Human Services.   III. Saint Paul
(Minn.)   IV. Ford Foundation.   V. Title: E.B.B.F.
HJ9156.E217   1984   352.1'4   84-13366
ISBN 0-8330-0582-0

The Rand Publication Series: The Report is the principal publication documenting and transmitting Rand's major research findings and final research results. The Rand Note reports other outputs of sponsored research for general distribution. Publications of The Rand Corporation do not necessarily reflect the opinions or policies of the sponsors of Rand research.

Published by The Rand Corporation

R-3124-HHS/SP/FF

EBBF

A Guide to Installing Equitable Beneficiary-Based Finance in Local Government

Anthony Pascal
With Michael Caggiano, Judith Fernandez,
Kevin McCarthy, Kevin Neels, C. Peter Rydell,
James P. Stucker

June 1984

Prepared for
The U.S. Department of Health
    and Human Services
The City of Saint Paul
The Ford Foundation

1700 MAIN STREET
P.O. BOX 2138
SANTA MONICA, CA 90406-2138

FOREWORD

Beneficiary charges are monies collected from the individual consumers of government services. An equitable beneficiary charge is one that minimizes adverse effects on the disadvantaged. The growing prominence of beneficiary charges in local government prompted a program of studies at Rand designed to explore the efficacy and equity of this method of financing public services.

We prepared the present Guide, with its summary of our findings, as an aid for local governments that may contemplate adopting the beneficiary-based finance (BBF) approach and therefore will have to deal with an array of questions and problems:

- The scope and nature of BBF
- Why local governments adopt BBF and why the pace of adoption has accelerated
- How to tell whether BBF has promise for a particular government
- The major advantages of BBF, and its disadvantages
- The services for which beneficiary charges are appropriate and inappropriate
- The way beneficiary charges are set, ideally and practically
- The kinds of organization and management reforms that should accompany the installation of BBF
- The potential inequities lurking in the BBF approach
- Ensuring equitable treatment by modifying the BBF approach—that is, prefixing an "E" to BBF
- Political and administrative problems in implementing EBBF

This Guide grew directly out of two projects recently completed by a team of Rand analysts. The first, for the City of Saint Paul, Minnesota, involved a fiscal diagnosis, the design of an overall approach to beneficiary charges, and the specifications for a new organizational form called the revenue center, which would levy the charges. Pilot demonstrations of the revenue center concept were developed for Saint Paul's traffic and lighting, and municipal athletic functions. The second project encompassed literature reviews, a survey of beneficiary charge practices across more than one hundred local government entities, and the analysis of the effects of beneficiary charges—both blanket charges and those with equity protections—for civil courts and emergency medical service, based on experience in a large urban county.

The body of this Guide consists of questions and brief answers about EBBF. Our aim is to lend practical assistance to local government officials and managers who are interested in exploring the promise of EBBF for their jurisdictions. Readers who need more technical detail may want to consult one of the following related Rand publications:

- *Exploring Benefit-Based Financing for Local Government Services: Must User Charges Harm the Disadvantaged?* N-2108-HHS, July 1984.
- *The Entrepreneurial City: Innovations in Finance and Management for Saint Paul,* R-3123-SP/FF, 1984.
- *How Trial Fees Would Affect Civil Justice,* P-6959, April 1984.
- *Five Year Revenue and Cost Forecasts for the City of Saint Paul,* N-2066-SP, April 1984.
- *The Post-Municipal City,* P-6792, July 1982.
- *Fiscal Restraints and the Burden of Local and State Taxes,* R-2646-FF/RC, August 1981.
- *How Fiscal Restraint Affects Spending and Services in Cities,* R-2644-FF/RC, January 1982.

A GUIDE TO INSTALLING EQUITABLE BENEFICIARY-BASED FINANCE IN LOCAL GOVERNMENT

WHAT IS MEANT BY "BENEFICIARY CHARGES"?

Beneficiary charges are amounts that consumers pay in direct exchange for government services received.

User charges (e.g., water bills, payments for using public tennis courts, transit fares, trash collection fees) are certainly the most typical. Very important, consumers can avoid charges by declining to use the service—a fact that, as we shall see, reduces the "waste" that occurs when services are "free" (that is, tax-supported).

But cities and counties impose many other fees that also fall under the rubric of beneficiary charges. Licenses and permits, for example, entail direct payments by consumers for services produced by the government—inspection, regulation, etc.

Special assessments, when properly tied to direct measures of benefits received, also count as beneficiary charges. An annual payment for street lighting service based on a combination of parcel front footage, spacing of light standards, and quality of equipment certainly extracts revenues from direct beneficiaries, even though no decline-to-consume option is offered. Periodic neighborhood votes on desired local lighting levels would go part of the way toward consumer choice, however. Property taxes, on the other hand, rise with property values rather than with receipt of services and thus are not beneficiary charges.

Earmarking—dedication of revenues to support the service subject to exaction—is a frequent but not invariable characteristic of beneficiary charges.

HOW DEPENDENT IS THE TYPICAL LOCAL GOVERNMENT ON BBF?

Cities now collect about 14 percent of their revenues in beneficiary charges; property taxes provide something like 22 percent, and grants from federal and state sources about 36 percent. (The rest comes from other local taxes and miscellaneous sources.) But over the past decade, beneficiary charge revenues have been growing about three times as fast as property tax levies. And, beginning in the late 1970s, the average city became less dependent on intergovernmental transfers as the inflation-adjusted value of grants began to fall rapidly. As a result, some cities now count on BBF for 30 to 40 percent of their revenues. Socially homogeneous cities of moderate size, especially in the West, tend to use BBF the most avidly. Cities in states with tough tax-cap laws are also heavy users.

Counties have pursued BBF almost as avidly, even though the concept is not appropriate for some of their chief activities—welfare, health, criminal justice. The beneficiary-charge/property-tax/grant breakdown for the typical county runs about 14 percent/26 percent/48 percent. Recently, however, BBF for counties has grown eight times as fast as county property tax collections.

WHY DO GOVERNMENTS ADOPT BBF?

Mostly because they need the money. Faced with cuts in grants from Washington and their state capitals, fiscal limits like Proposition 13 and Proposition 2-1/2, and fears that raising the unpopular property tax will provoke taxpayer flight, leaders have been turning to consumer charges to bail out the public treasury. New charges can generate sizable revenues.

But there are other good reasons. BBF imposes costs directly on those who benefit. This has two desirable effects:

- People use public resources more prudently when they have to pay for waste or misuse. Meter-based water charges prompt people to repair leaky faucets. Greens fees will induce golfers to limit their time on public courses.
- The resulting system conforms to traditional notions of fairness: "Pay for what you get." Allocation of burdens to users achieves more equity in the horizontal sense; that is, citizens of equal socioeconomic status will pay for public service according to their consumption. (But BBF may require adjustments to preserve vertical equity, which is based on ability to pay.)

And polls reveal that Americans prefer charges to taxes. That preference points to a problem. Charges are most efficient, equitable, and preferable when they replace taxes; because they raise additional revenue, however, only when added on top of taxes, revenue-raising conflicts with the other objectives.

Finally, BBF can promote important improvements in the operating efficiency of the agencies that use it. It promotes businesslike management in government because it focuses attention on consumer satisfaction and the "bottom line." Below, we suggest some organizational reforms—under the revenue center concept—for enhancing the payoff from BBF.

ARE THERE ANY DISADVANTAGES TO BBF?

Yes—but the main ones are remediable.

The first disadvantage stems from the new fiscal burdens that undifferentiated BBF may impose on the poor and other disadvantaged groups. Such people are now asked to pay for services that they traditionally received "free" (meaning supported by taxpayers).

That fact raises a further question: Won't the switchover to BBF make government too much like business, its leaders too much like entrepreneurs? The answer is no, if the system is properly structured and appropriately monitored. The pursuit of social objectives, rather than simple moneymaking, will stay in the forefront if service managers are given the right incentives and the central leadership maintains the right controls.

Administration, collection, and maintenance costs will make some beneficiary charges infeasible. Fine. That simply means that those services should not be subject to charge, however justifiable they may be on other grounds. No one is proposing coin-operated turnstiles to control the use of public sidewalks, or toll booths at city street intersections.

In general, the distribution of economic welfare will shift as service users assume burdens that historically have been imposed on the general taxpayer. This shift may generate the chief political obstacle.

DOES YOUR GOVERNMENT NEED BBF?

The superiority of the beneficiary charge approach seems obvious for certain kinds of services. Discouraging the less avid users, allocating the burdens to responsible parties, and promoting internal efficiencies in delivery are worthy objectives for any government. Practically speaking, however, the more fiscal pressure you face, the more likely you are to be interested in the new revenues available through BBF.

How Can You Tell Whether Your Jurisdiction Faces a Long-run Fiscal Problem?

Fiscal forecasts play an important role in strategic planning. They depict a jurisdiction's financial future. They can show a city or county where it is going, given its current policies and assuming business as usual. Today's discovery of impending shortfalls will inspire actions to stave them off. Steady or, even worse, expanding shortfalls in out-years imply a structural defect in the jurisdiction's fiscal base that is probably going to require a structural remedy. (See N-2066-SP, the Rand forecast publication for Saint Paul, cited in the Foreword.)

To produce a fiscal prognosis, you will need independent projections of revenues and expenditures. Even though most local governments cannot legally operate with deficits, making separate forecasts will show the size of the future problem which, if not cured, will require tax increases, service cutbacks, or some other stopgap measures.

What Do Revenue Forecasts Entail?

Group your revenue sources into categories that reflect the driving factors causing change. Driving factors are of two general sorts: background and policy. Background factors tend to be economic or demographic. For instance, property tax revenue will rise along with property values (if not legally capped), sales tax revenues with retail sales, other revenues with population or payrolls or some other factor. The rate of inflation, you will find, plays the dominant role for many revenue services.

Important policy factors include state aid formulas, tax limitation formulas, variations in federal or state grants, revenue sharing, and the like. The formula-related sources, being easy enough to forecast, call for no further comment. Projecting state and federal aids that are determined by annual appropriation may require a scenario approach, using best guesses from such sources as the U.S. Office of Management and Budget and the Congressional Budget Office.

You are now ready to combine the forecasts driven by background and by policy factors to produce an overall revenue projection. A single forecast is not enough, however, because it cannot embody all of the true uncertainties the future holds. You will probably want to work with rates of inflation that are higher and lower (as measured by the annual rate of increase in the Consumer Price Index, CPI) than the "official" forecasts. Most of the other economic factors will move with inflation and should be adjusted upward or downward for the high-inflation and low-inflation cases. Similarly, "generous" and "stingy" scenarios, to flank the most likely cases, should be developed for state and federal grants.

What Do Expenditure Forecasts Involve?

They are somewhat simpler. Since you want to know the effects of continuing on the current course, you merely need to establish the future cost of the quantities of inputs you use, including plans on the books for capital improvements. For personnel, the most straightforward procedure assumes the continuation of today's real value of wages and fringes; you therefore inflate the compensation package by the alternative inflation rates used in the revenue projections. For nonpersonnel costs, use recent relationships between general inflation and price trends for other relevant goods and services. Make sure you apply an interest rate that is consistent with each of the alternative inflation rates when figuring interest expense for newly floated bond issues in future years.

What Conditions Lead to Structural Budget Shortfalls?

A forecasted rate of expenditure growth that exceeds the forecasted rate of revenue growth presages a budget shortfall. The operational implications can be expressed in a number of ways to make the meaning of the shortfall more concrete. For example:

- Calculate the percentage increase in the property tax required to strike a balance between revenues and expenditures.
- Compute the across-the-board reduction in the workforce that would be necessary to close the gap. Using average compensation in each department, you can easily find the required workforce reduction when cuts are restricted to certain functions, too.
- Reckon the reduction in the real value of the wage-and-fringe bill necessary to balance the budget in future year x.

And remember that expedients such as these—one-shot tax increases, service cutbacks, or wage reductions—will not stem a widening shortfall. To solve that sort of structural problem, you need a permanent and expanding source of new revenues. In that situation, BBF may prove the superior solution.

But for various reasons, BBF may not be applicable to all services. We turn now to some of those reasons.

SHOULD GOVERNMENTS TRY TO APPLY BBF ACROSS THE BOARD?

Certainly not. Services that governments provide differ dramatically in their intended purposes and patterns of consumption. These variations will affect the applicability of the BBF concept.

For Example, Are Services with Heavy Public Good Content Amenable to BBF?

Not very. "Public good" services (to use the economists' term) are those whose benefits are largely indivisible among consumers. This means there is no practical way to exclude anyone from enjoying the benefits of the service. Think of crime prevention and law enforcement. The police function serves the citizenry as a whole; if anyone enjoys the benefits, it means that all enjoy the benefits. Fire prevention, the control of land use, the suppression of communicable diseases, and the facilitation and control of street traffic also generate indivisible benefits. Services with substantial "public good" components, then, are the least amenable to BBF.

Our survey of jurisdictions confirmed this proposition. Police and fire departments garner only a negligible part of their budgets in the form of consumer fees. They often charge for special services (records reproduction, safety inspections, special event security) where the beneficiary can be identified, but the bulk of their revenues comes from the general fund (made up of property taxes, utility taxes, grants, etc.).

BBF may occasionally be appropriate, however, even in the case of protective services and public works. Buildings that threaten to make extraordinary demands on the safety services—perhaps because they are large, or old, or deteriorated, or lack devices for alarm and detection or integral protection—might be assigned an extra burden in the form of an annual service charge or special assessment. When benefits received are not related simply to property values, special assessment may provide a superior method for the assignment of burdens. The special assessment route offers an additional bonus: Parcels exempt from the property tax—for instance those owned by nonprofit groups or other levels of government—can be tapped.

Growing communities often find it necessary to make major additions to capital plant to accommodate new developments, as for streets and public buildings. To cover necessary costs, many now levy fees on developers (who then recover them from eventual buyers of the new houses or stores or factories). Development fees are particularly popular where property tax lids are in force.

What About Services Specifically Intended To Help the Disadvantaged?

Applying BBF to such services defeats their purpose. Many social services, health care to indigents, public housing, and the like were deliberately intended as in-kind transfers to the less fortunate. BBF would simply take part of them back.

Some Services Have Little Public Good Content and Are Consumed by Rich and Poor Alike; Is BBF Suitable for Them?

Yes, they are the most amenable to the beneficiary charge approach. Governments provide "private good" services—in which individual beneficiaries are identifiable and do not consist exclusively of the disadvantaged—for two basic reasons:

(1) To be efficient, the service needs to function as a monopoly and the government must either operate or regulate such natural monopolies. (Think of water supply and sewer systems and, less strictly, refuse collection and mass transit.)

(2) The service may operate as an adjunct to or as a joint product with another service that does have high public good content. (Think of adult recreation and athletic programs conducted in city parks, and emergency medical (paramedic) services provided by firefighters.) Also important, private market substitutes for such services usually exist.

For all of these government-provided services, indivisible types of benefits are not paramount. Our survey revealed that water and sewer systems rely on consumer charges more often than any other local public services. Refuse collection (for which contracting out is also common) is the next most reliant on BBF. Although we did not survey transit services, fare-box finance is obviously common. BBF is prevalent, though far from universal, in recreation and emergency medical services. Many governments of course do not impose beneficiary charges even for their private good services; they continue to subsidize consumption out of tax revenues.

Does BBF Make Sense in the Case of Services with Mixed Public and Private Good Components?

Yes, but for these so-called merit goods (in the economists' jargon), charges should cover only the share of the benefit that is truly private. Prime examples of mixed services are parks and libraries. Such services produce benefits for individual consumers and for the wider community simultaneously. Visitors enjoy parks but so do nearby residents and even passersby. Borrowers benefit from public libraries but so does the public at large as its members become better informed and more enlightened. (In this sense libraries are like public education.) In neither of these mixed cases are beneficiary charges now much used, according to our survey of cities and counties.

Of course, it would be expensive to regulate admissions to parks—and inefficient in the short run to the extent that the park was not congested to begin with. You might need fences and toll gates. But an even more important deterrent to charging is the difficulty of isolating the private good component that ought to be imposed on the users. Or, to look at it from the other end: What subsidy should the general fund pay?

We still lack methods for finding the technically correct solution, but some rough-and-ready help comes from a procedure adapted from the deliberations of a citizens' advisory group appointed by the Mayor of Saint Paul. Ask the following questions about the service you have in mind, and when the answer is yes give it the points that follow the question:

Is it hard to identify individual beneficiaries? ...... 35 points

Is there a substantial community benefit? .... 30 points

Would there be considerable political opposition
    to user charges? .... 20 points

Would charges generate negligible revenues? .... 15 points

Sum up the points and you have a useful indication of the fraction of the cost of the service that the general fund might support—what we could call the proper public good subsidy for mixed services.

HOW SHOULD BENEFICIARY CHARGES BE SET?

Again, it depends on the type of service. Different charge procedures are appropriate for different services.

Isn't Cost Recovery the Most Common Base for Charges?

Yes, but it's not that simple. First, it requires a rather sophisticated cost accounting system to discover what your full costs really are.

Many existing systems provide no way to allocate capital, administrative, and overhead costs to specific services, for example. In the long run, the price per unit of service should equal the addition to full costs occasioned by the last unit produced.

Second, you will want to deduct the public good subsidy we just discussed for the mixed services. Ultimately, the aggregate charge to consumers for a given service should cover the difference between full costs and this subsidy from the general fund.

Third, the amount of service consumed is likely to fall as the price charged for it rises. Projections of long-run revenues from beneficiary charges must take this factor into account. Of course, the resulting change in service output can also affect cost of production, as time goes on (because the scale of operations changes). Lacking extensive market research, public managers must carefully track their "sales" against their "prices" and use these observations to determine the tradeoff between them. (Economists call this estimating the elasticity of demand.) Data on volume vs. costs are also worth collecting.

Fourth, for certain services, bases other than full cost may be preferable. Some alternatives follow.

For Which Services Is Market Pricing a Good Method?

Those that have close market alternatives. Most likely, these will include the private good services and those mixed services that are heavy on the private good side. Paramedic fees, for example, cannot greatly exceed those for similar services offered by private ambulance companies, nor is there much reason why they should fall far short. The same stricture would apply to tennis, golf, and swimming lessons provided by recreation departments. Suppose libraries began to charge fees to borrowers. Amounts would have to be sensitive to rental charges obtaining at private lending libraries and even to prices at paperback bookstores. In the case of private good services, when the government finds it cannot cover costs by charging market prices, it ought to consider turning the service over to private producers. For mixed services this criterion applies only to the private good component, of course.

Is Revenue Maximization Ever Appropriate?

Hardly ever. Governments provide monopoly services precisely to prevent revenue maximization (which can become price-gouging) by the supplier. However, public bodies do sometimes tack a small markup onto their monopoly services. That is, they charge a fee that exceeds the full long-run unit costs. The extra revenues then go to subsidize other services. Markups also serve to exact revenues from residents and institutions not subject to the property tax.

WHAT ARE THE ORGANIZATIONAL IMPLICATIONS OF A SWITCH TO BBF?

The BBF approach can work within the traditional structure of local government. Departments and bureaus would go on providing public services as they always have, but would apply beneficiary charges where deemed appropriate, as described earlier. However, certain kinds of reorganization can greatly enhance the advantages of BBF. The chief new departure in organization is the establishment of "revenue centers." (R-3123-SP/FF, *The Entrepreneurial City*, contains a good deal of detail on this innovation.)

How Would Establishing "Revenue Centers" Enhance BBF?

Revenue centers are new organizational entities that produce private good services, which they sell to the city's consumers, and public good services on contract with the central administration. They combine the characteristics of an enterprise fund in public administration and those of a profit center in a large corporation (like the Chevrolet Division of the General Motors Corporation). That is, they conduct a number of selected functions, collect various kinds of revenues, and operate in a semiautonomous fashion. Their performance is assessed on the basis of a "bottom line"—that is, they strive for self-support, or even an excess of revenues over costs that leads to an earned surplus.

What Functions Should Be Grouped into a Revenue Center?

Broadly, two choices are available. Revenue centers can span services that use similar means of production—for instance, the various aspects of recreation, or services devoted to particular constituencies—for instance, the elderly. The first criterion usually defines the organization in traditional local governments and is probably superior for revenue centers as well. Concentrating on production commonalities plays to staff knowledge built up over the years on how to get things done. The advantage of the user-orientation lies in its focus on markets; it keeps the revenue center attuned to opportunities for expanding its product line. Generally, then, the current organization will suggest appropriate groupings for revenue centers. Once off and running, however, centers will add new services as openings appear and drop old services for which production costs or demand conditions bode ill, at least in the case of private good services.

Revenue centers are not restricted to the provision of private good or mixed services. They use their skill in production (or marketing) to offer an array of related services in which they have the comparative advantage. These may well include public goods and redistributive goods that share inputs (or customers) with their marketed goods. Different kinds of revenues flow from each type of service.

How Do Revenue Centers Finance Themselves?

For private good services and the private component of mixed services, the revenues derive from charges, fees, assessments, and other prices imposed on beneficiaries. Earmarked taxes—for example, on gasoline sales, dedicated to street maintenance—would also accrue to some revenue centers and would be treated much like user charges. The centers, in addition, collect the subsidies provided by the general fund, set to cover public good and redistributive objectives.

The production of public good and redistributive services with the general fund as a client might be characterized as a process of "contracting in" (as opposed to contracting out, where the public agency hires a private firm). Under contracting in, the central administration directs the revenue center to produce an agreed-upon level of service in exchange for a multiyear grant. The size of the grant will depend on historical costs of production. The central administration must also institute procedures to ensure compliance with quantity and quality standards for the service contracted in.

Finally, revenue centers will derive additional income from business ventures, many of which will consist of sales of service to other governmental jurisdictions in the area. In many cases, you should expect opposition by competitive private businesses, in the form of political pressure. Once incentives for expansion come into force, center employees and managers will discover new opportunities to market, say, parking meter maintenance, or forensic lab services, or firefighter training courses to neighboring municipalities, or to the county.

To produce the right incentives, revenues generated by the centers must accrue to the center's own budget. It should see itself as master of its own fate. If the revenue center can also retain a share of any surpluses it earns, it will work harder to control costs. But just as full revenues must be credited to the center, so must full costs. Fringes, bills for support services, contributions to overhead, and charges for capital depletion should be charged against the center.

How Do Revenue Centers Affect Management in Local Government?

Revenue centers will see their role as fulfilling the demands for service in the markets they operate in. They will begin to treat residents more as customers and less as wards. Revenue expansion, cost containment, and capital preservation will become management goals. Budgetary politics will recede in importance.

Surpluses retained in revenue centers might go for a variety of purposes:

- To finance new equipment;
- To provide seed capital for new ventures;
- For employee training and staff development programs;
- As merit pay for people whose actions made a noticeable contribution to the earning of the surplus.

Particularly successful centers should not be singled out for cuts in the contracting-in arrangement; that would destroy incentives for increased productivity. However, some agreed-upon share of surpluses should be periodically returned to the general fund so as to prevent uncontrolled growth in the function performed by the center. These surpluses can help finance public good and redistributive services or serve to reduce taxes.

Revenue center managers should have wide latitude to initiate new lines of activity that make no call on general fund support. However, managers should be required to submit plans that project expected revenues and expenditures. And ventures that do not succeed deserve expeditious termination.

In many cities and counties, a revenue center style of operation may require alterations in staffing procedures. Rigid civil service rules or restrictive collective bargaining agreements may inhibit the flexibility and responsiveness required in the new, more dynamic environment. Some workers may need counseling and reassurance after years of working in the predictable world of general fund support.

What Will the Revenue Center Approach Mean for Accountability?

Revenue centers should develop in those agencies where expertise and the need to be responsive to consumer desires promise more efficiency and more citizen satisfaction. But installing centers need not compromise accountability. Central authority—the chief executive and legislative body—will still call the necessary shots and will continue to provide leadership. A number of features of the approach assure this outcome. They bear reiterating:

- The contracting-in agreements—periodically renegotiated—will govern the provision of public good services and will affect the supply of mixed services.
- Central authorities will regulate prices charged by the monopoly services.
- Arrangements for sharing of revenue center surpluses will change as underlying conditions shift.
- Loans by revenue centers from the general fund or from other revenue centers will require approval. To obtain outside resources, the centers will have to rely on the bonding powers of the city or county.
- The reserve authority of the central administration will continue to prevail; power to approve budgets and, in fact, the threat of intervention in any aspect of center relations will tend to keep the centers in line.

So revenue centers provide an attractive vehicle for instituting BBF. We must still ask whether a beneficiary charge system can be adjusted to reflect ability to pay.

CAN BBF BE MODIFIED TO PROTECT THE DISADVANTAGED?

A number of devices are available and are in fact used. Local leaders, after all, seek ways to mitigate the new fiscal burdens that beneficiary charges could impose on low-income groups. These equity protections are what put the "E" in EBBF.

They take three essential forms. The first is an assurance of the continuing provision of public good and explicitly redistributive services. The second involves manipulation of the charge structure for mixed and private good services to ease the burdens placed on the less fortunate. The third is a comprehensive voucher system.

How Does BBF Work to Assure the Availability of Basic Services to All?

The establishment of beneficiary charges in local government helps guarantee that the resources will be available to support continued provision of basic government services to all members of the community. The "free" (i.e., tax-financed) basic services take two important forms:

public-good type services such as law enforcement and fire prevention, and redistributive type services such as public assistance, health clinics, and social services. The more that mixed and private-type services are supported by beneficiary charges, the more tax resources are available to finance these basic services. Continuation of tax-supported basic services constitutes the first line of defense for the disadvantaged.

Can Beneficiary Charges Be Adjusted to Reduce Inequity?

Even in cases where fees and charges are imposed, it is often possible to make adjustments that reduce their inequitable effects. Such built-in protections comprise the second line of defense for disadvantaged groups.

Lifeline Rates. One approach is a variant on lifeline electricity rates. The idea is to charge a low price for some minimum level of consumption. Above that level, the price per unit rises. As a result, poor families in small houses with few appliances pay low rates, while wealthier families in large, well-equipped houses pay more.

Our survey of beneficiary charge practices turned up several examples of this form of protection for disadvantaged service users. Municipally owned utilities have lifeline rate structures for electricity, water, and sewer service. Refuse collection fee structures offer free or cheap service for the first two trash containers and charge more for additional service.

Target Group Discounts. A second approach is built on the example of the special fares for various eligible groups used on public transit systems. Group discounts are potentially relevant to a variety of city services in which residents pay a fee at the point of use.

The elderly are often the beneficiaries of group discount schemes. Examples range from drainage fees to library charges to emergency medical service subscriptions. Other groups singled out include children and the disabled. Some charge systems favor residences over business firms and nonprofit groups over ordinary enterprises. Accepting that the poor are more likely to delay paying user-charge bills, many jurisdictions deliberately make little attempt to collect on delinquent accounts.

Neighborhood Rebates. Still another approach incorporates charges that vary with the income of the neighborhood. Rebates in low-income neighborhoods (identified, say, through census tract statistics) could offset fees for local facilities such as libraries and health clinics, or for such services as recreation and street sweeping.

Surprisingly, our survey uncovered no cases where charges varied with neighborhood socioeconomic characteristics (although there were cases in which special assessments did). The fear of strong political reaction to such obvious differentiation probably explains it.

Special Assessment Deferrals. For services financed through special assessments—examples might include street maintenance and lighting, and neighborhood parks—governments can grant disadvantaged homeowners the option of deferring payment so that the assessments accumulate as a lien on the property. In this way the jurisdiction avoids placing undue burdens on homeowners with limited cash income. Deferral plans are growing in popularity.

The initiation of deferrals will cause a temporary dip in assessment revenues, but the natural rate of property turnover will soon bring collections back to normal. Imposing a market rate of interest on the liens will make it possible to offer the deferral option to all assessees, not only the disadvantaged. Universalizing the deferral option would eliminate the administrative costs associated with determining eligibility.

What Problems Are Presented by Equity Adjustments to Beneficiary Charges?

Whether a jurisdiction opts for lifeline rates or group discounts or neighborhood rebates, a "fair" subsidy level will have to be established. At what level of use do lifeline rates no longer apply? What shall be the discount on library membership fees for senior citizens? If a neighborhood has two-thirds the city's average household income, should its recreation centers impose charges only two-thirds of the standard? How should the city or county government define disadvantage? By age? By handicap? By income? If it chooses the last, how will it certify eligibility? These are largely political judgments; the city or county government must decide how generous it wants to be and to whom.

Moreover, none of the devices or combinations will produce perfect targeting. Some rich people live in poor neighborhoods and vice versa. Not all the elderly are disadvantaged. Some affluent households will use so little of a service that they never exceed the lifeline level, and some poor households may be so large that they pay the premium rates. Deferred special assessments will constitute a burden when properties eventually turn over. In other words, the ad hoc equity protections cannot be sufficiently inclusive nor can they target with much accuracy.

Can a Supervoucher Scheme Solve these Problems?

The most comprehensive and precise method for maintaining access to city services under BBF is a system of Supervouchers, financed from the jurisdiction's general revenues. Such a scheme would make lump-sum grants available in the form of vouchers that members of disadvantaged groups could use to purchase a wide range of public services that are subject to charge or assessment. The household would select among the array of available services until it exhausted its grant. The Supervoucher fund would compensate government departments for services provided to eligible users.

In developing a Supervoucher system, three design issues in particular require resolution: eligibility, form of payment, and accountability.

The jurisdiction will have to establish eligibility for receipt of vouchers. When not defined in terms of easily verifiable characteristics such as age, physical handicap, or residence address—for example, if income becomes the criterion—a practical way of screening applicants is necessary. Jurisdiction-administered means tests are expensive and often demeaning to applicants. But Supervoucher eligibility could depend on the acceptance of certifications by county or state or federal government for other purposes, such as public assistance, Medicaid, food stamps, school lunch, or unemployment compensation.

As to forms of payment, Supervouchers could use scrip that would be exchangeable for the services subject to charge, or special credit cards, with charges deducted from a household's Supervoucher account. Agencies providing services would receive reimbursement on presentation of the scrip or verification of credit card transactions.

The potential for overdrafts and the possibility of use by ineligibles would call for some policing. A secondary market in scrip could develop, as it has for food stamps.

The technical feasibility of the Supervoucher system has not yet been tested or demonstrated. Each jurisdiction would need to determine for itself whether the benefits would outweigh the administrative costs, and think over the political reaction such an explicit redistribution policy might provoke.

How Much Might the Installation of Equity Protections Cost?

Rand performed three case studies to analyze the feasibility of adjusting charges to protect the disadvantaged. One study was of emergency medical assistance, which commonly uses BBF; in the other two, civil courts and traffic and street lighting, beneficiary charges are much less common.

Emergency Medical Service. We concluded that in a large urban county, institution of emergency medical service (EMS) charges at a level close to full cost recovery would raise about $4 million per year, and would reduce EMS calls by about one-third.

Because low-income people make more use of EMS (at least for non-cardiac, non-accident cases), we also calculated the effects of charge rebates in the poorest fifth of all census tracts: a $1 million reduction in revenue and a 12 percent increase in runs as compared with a charge-but-no-rebate system. Other aspects of EMS operation also affect the equity of the system. For example, when service includes transportation to the hospital, EMS charges will show up on the hospital bill and thus become reimbursable by insurance carriers or Medicare/Medicaid. EMS charges that add a premium for the more expensive forms of treatment, such as cardiac cases, are more advantageous to low-income people who tend not to make disproportionate use of that category of care. (See Rand Note N-2108-HHS, *Exploring Benefit-Based Financing*, as listed in the Foreword.)

Civil Courts. Shrinking tax revenues and rising costs have led civil court agencies to consider consumer charges. In a large jurisdiction, the average civil trial might cost the taxpayers about $2700. Our case study demonstrated that if plaintiffs and defendants were to split that cost, the new revenues would cover about a quarter of the superior court budget and that the number of civil trials would decline by about 25 percent. (More cases would be settled out of court.) Fewer trials mean less court congestion, trial delay, and juror payments and, in the long run, fewer required judges and courtrooms. Gains and losses to the various participants in the system would change only negligibly as a result of trial fees because so few cases come to trial anyway and because trial costs are swamped by lawyers' costs.

Exempting low-income plaintiffs from trial fees—a deliberate equity protection—would cost taxpayers about $1.2 million a year in lost revenues and would raise trial frequency slightly as compared with a situation with trial fees and no exemptions. Interestingly, low-income plaintiffs would better their economic situations in a fee-with-exemptions system because they would be in a stronger bargaining position vis-a-vis defendants. (See N-2108-HHS, *Exploring Benefit-Based Financing*.)

Traffic and Lighting Functions. We designed a revenue center and a set of new charges, including special assessments, for the traffic and lighting functions in Saint Paul. The result was a shift from 80-percent dependence on the general fund to only 20 percent. The proposed residential street lighting assessment would be based on both level and quality of service received by the individual household. It would recover the full cost of lighting but would contain an interest-generating deferral option, available to all residents. Assessments, under the deferral plan, would begin to approach a steady state in revenues produced by about the tenth year of the program. (See R-3123-SP/FF, *The Entrepreneurial City*.)

WHAT ARE THE PREREQUISITES FOR EFFECTIVE IMPLEMENTATION OF EBBF?

There are several and they span different activities—public relations, data collection, political decisions, and experimentation.

What Kind of Public Relations Groundwork Is Required?

Many different groups could initially oppose the imposition of benefit-based finance. Taxpayers might feel disinclined to paying more. Public employees might resist switching to an unfamiliar and less predictable method of operation. Advocates of the poor might fear a move toward regressivity. Politicians might fight the loss of control inherent in financing public service through collections from consumers rather than through appropriations decisions of legislators.

The first and most general requirement is that the advocates of EBBF feel secure about its advantages—the kind of armament this Guide has sought to provide in earlier sections.

As to taxpayer concerns, whether beneficiary charges constitute replacements for or additions to taxes will largely depend on the revenue situation of the adopting jurisdiction. The more that charges replace taxes, of course, the more efficiency in consumption and production they bring about. Good government and taxpayer organizations should thus favor beneficiary charges, at least when they substitute for property and other local taxes. But EBBF can help raise additional revenues when the only alternative is a drastic cutback in public services.

The reply to employees' worries is twofold, again paralleling the two objectives of beneficiary charges. When the charges are designed to raise new revenues, they may actually save civil service jobs threatened by budget shortfalls. More callous, if no less true, is the second reply: Enhanced efficiency often carries the burden of additional risk. This is not to say that governments should not try to ease the transition to a more entrepreneurial environment. Some employees—staff and management both—will actually welcome the opportunity to innovate that EBBF brings.

The devices designed to minimize vertical inequities require sophisticated and effective articulation. Promulgators of EBBF must be prepared to show how the reforms they propose do in fact maintain fairness through built-in equity protections. In many cases the need for explicit protection devices is obviated by a showing that disadvantaged groups are not frequent users of the public service for which charges are contemplated, or at least not as frequent as might have been thought.

For the concerns of politicians, there are no completely satisfactory replies. Loss of control may well occur. We might add, however, that the loss of political control over private good services seems justified. (The competing solution, after all, is to simply privatize them.) And some control will persist through mayor and council input into capital allocation procedures, personnel code enforcement, and the fixing of subsidy levels for those services that have public good content or call for guaranteed access by the disadvantaged.

What Are the Data Requirements for Installation of EBBF?

Good financial systems require good data. For an equitable benefit-based system, the data requirements weigh heavier still.

Full Cost Accounting. In calculating beneficiary charges, knowing the true cost of the service marks the starting point. The costs of capital and a fair share of overhead and other forms of administration must be allocated to each service. If producers and consumers do not know the full resource cost of the service provided, they cannot make rational decisions about how much to produce and consume. Many existing municipal and county systems lack the cost-accounting capability that would produce the numbers necessary to set effective charges.

Knowledge of Markets. Charge designers need to know market conditions for the service in question for at least two reasons. First, revenue forecasting requires estimates of the relation between price and quantity consumed. How many fewer library memberships will be sold as the membership fee climbs from x to y dollars per year?

Second, a public service may have such a close private-market substitute that charges for the former need to be sensitive to prices for the latter. Think of paramedic vs. private ambulance services, public library books vs. books from lending libraries, municipal golf courses vs. private golf courses.

The Incidence of Consumption. The quantity of a service that a target-group uses—the "incidence of consumption"—is also important. To gauge the desirability of protection devices, you need to know how imposing a charge on the item in question would affect the budgets of target-group households. If the effect is trivial, the inequity can probably be ignored. Then, too, summing up levels of consumption across all of the services subject to charge yields an upper bound to the drawing rights under the Supervoucher scheme.

Defining Target Group Eligibles. Planners will have to determine which persons, or households, in the community are eligible for equity protections. It is easy enough to ascertain age and address, although even for these attributes, misrepresentation is possible. Determining income or physical disability poses tougher problems. The best solution might depend on kicking the problem upstairs. Eligibility for discounts or deferrals or Supervouchers could piggyback on certifications of disadvantage made by other levels of government.

What Are the Key Political Decisions?

Three basic problems demand resolution, but there are no ready technical solutions because they all require data unlikely to be available, or pure political input. A lively debate among interest groups, say through representatives on a mayor's task force or advisory panel, might be the best vehicle for making these decisions.

Determining the Public Good Subsidy for Each Government Service. Theoretically, we could ascertain the social as opposed to the individual consumer's benefit of after-school recreation programs. It would require determining the reduction in juvenile delinquency associated with participation in city park athletic leagues, and the dollar cost of juvenile crime to the community. Similarly with fire service (the value to the public of preventing a spreading conflagration vs. the value to the homeowner of saving his or her dwelling), library service (the value of a better educated citizenry vs. an individual reader's enjoyment of books), and trash collection (a tidy and sanitary community vs. convenience to individual householders). But practically, no such information exists. Instead, rough-and-ready procedures will apply, perhaps as sketched out earlier.

Defining Eligibility for Equity Protection. Rules on eligibility also need drafting. Should the poor be protected? What about the old, even if not poor? Children? To what age? How serious a handicap qualifies a person as disabled? Again, chief executives and constituted legislative bodies may want to consult citizen task forces when resolving such issues.

Deciding on the Amount of Equity Protection. It is still not enough to know which services will qualify for equity protection and who may receive it. The magnitude of protection also has to be established. What will be the total Supervoucher drawing rights for a family of four with an income of $10,000? What are the proper lifeline rates for trash collection? Senior discounts at the library? Swimming pool rebates in poor neighborhoods?

Could Demonstrations and Experiments Help Refine the EBBF Approach?

Yes. Equitable benefit-based finance is new, not all the answers are available, and experimentation is therefore appropriate. Along with an experimental attitude goes a commitment to systematic evaluation and a readiness to make revisions when they seem advisable. For some services, for example, high administrative or collection costs may make the EBBF approach not worth pursuing. Revenues may fail to meet projections or, just as embarrassing, may too greatly surpass them. Managers may set charges so as to exploit a monopoly situation. Political reactions to neighborhood rebates may be so sharp as to invalidate the notion. Revenue centers may fail to pursue social objectives. Insufficient equity protection may inflame disadvantaged consumers. Employee morale may wane.

Continuing evaluations will reveal such problems. Independent appraisals should gauge success and failure of the various experiments through objective examination of data on costs, effects, coverage, access, and satisfaction. Reactions of consumers, managers, and workers should be monitored. You will want to contrast the experimental charge systems and the revenue center approach with the traditional method of service provision, that is, through tax support of conventional agencies.

Boldness in instituting beneficiary charges and revenue centers should be matched by boldness in revising plans where they prove intractable or infeasible or perverse in their effects. A spirit of pragmatism will help bring about the fiscal amplitude, operating efficiency, and fair treatment that EBBF so enticingly promises.

ACKNOWLEDGMENTS

The following organizations contributed to the support of the research on which this publication is based:

The United States Department of Health and Human Services, Office of Human Development Services

The Ford Foundation

The United States Department of Housing and Urban Development, Office of Policy Development and Research

The Saint Paul Companies

The General Mills Foundation

The Saint Paul Foundation

The F. R. Bigelow Foundation

The Otto Bremer Foundation

A Rand team worked intensively, under contract, with leaders, managers, employees, and citizens in Saint Paul, Minnesota, developing many of the ideas presented here and helping establish pilot demonstrations. Los Angeles County officials, especially in the Chief Administrative Office and Fire Department, provided some advice and data, although the County was not a sponsor of the studies.

We particularly thank Mayor George Latimer, Peter Hames, and Susan Job of Saint Paul, Lloyd Halstead of Los Angeles County, James Dolson of HHS, Louis Winnick and David Arnold of The Ford Foundation, and Charles Smith and Henry Felder of HUD for their counsel and encouragement. John Goering served as HUD project monitor.

A National Advisory Panel, composed of local government leaders, assembled twice to comment on the Rand work. Its members were Vincent Cianci, Mayor of Providence; Donald Fraser, Mayor of Minneapolis; Walter Tucker, Mayor of Compton, California; John Collins, City of Seattle; James Etheredge, City of Charleston, South Carolina; Charles Hill, City of Phoenix; James Rich, City of Seattle; and Thomas Smerling, City of Minneapolis. We are grateful for their help.

Others of our Rand colleagues made important contributions to the research. They include Susan Bell, Mark Boyce, Stephen Carroll, Jane Cobb, Carol Hillestad, James Kakalik, and Sally Trude. Daniel Kohler and Timothy Quinn reviewed a manuscript version of this Guide and offered important suggestions for improvement. David Lyon, Vice President of Rand's Domestic Research Division, provided advice and support.

INDEX